LIFE'S LITTLE BOOK OF
WISDOM FOR
Teachers

Published by Barbour Publishing, Inc., P.O. Box 719, Uhrichsville, Ohio 44683,
www.barbourbooks.com

Our mission is to publish and distribute inspirational products offering exceptional value and biblical encouragement to the masses.

 Member of the
Evangelical Christian
Publishers Association

Printed in China.

Life's Little Book of
Wisdom for
Teachers

BARBOUR
PUBLISHING

We make a living by what we get;
we make a life by what we give.

WINSTON CHURCHILL

When we take time to notice the simple things in life, we never lack for encouragement. We discover we are surrounded by limitless hope that's just wearing everyday clothes.

ANONYMOUS

Every now and then go away, have a little relaxation, for when you come back to your work, your judgment will be surer. Go some distance away, because then the work appears smaller and more of it can be taken in at a glance and a lack of harmony and proportion is more readily seen.

LEONARDO DA VINCI

Well done is better than well said.

BENJAMIN FRANKLIN

A teacher affects eternity:
He can never tell where his influence stops.

HENRY ADAMS

A word fitly spoken is like
apples of gold in pictures of silver.

PROVERBS 25:11

To find joy in work is to discover the fountain of youth.

PEARL S. BUCK

What nobler profession than to touch
the next generation—to see children hold
your understanding in their eyes, your hope
in their lives, your world in their hands.
In their success you find your own,
and so to them you give your all.

UNKNOWN

Anyone who keeps learning stays young.

HENRY FORD

Words, when well chosen,
have so great a force in them that a
description often gives us more lively
ideas than the sight of things themselves.

JOSEPH ADDISON

What teachers instill in young minds
is the spark from which generations
of flaming torches of truth may be lit.

COLLEEN L. REECE AND ANITA CORRINE DONIHUE

Great people are those who can
make others feel that they,
too, can become great.

MARK TWAIN

The mind is not a vessel to be filled,
but a fire to be ignited.

PLUTARCH

A soft answer turneth away wrath:
but grievous words stir up anger.

PROVERBS 15:1

A pessimist sees the difficulty in every opportunity; an optimist sees the opportunity in every difficulty.

WINSTON CHURCHILL

Education. . .is a painful, continual,
and difficult work to be done in kindness,
by watching, by warning. . .by praise,
but above all—by example.

JOHN RUSKIN

*Children have more need
of models than of critics.*

JOSEPH JOUBERT

Correction does much,
but encouragement does more.

JOHANN WOLFGANG VON GOETHE

May He support us all the day long,
till the shadows lengthen, and the evening
comes, and the busy world is hushed,
and the fever of life is over, and our work
is done! Then in His mercy may He give us
a safe lodging, and a holy rest,
and peace at the last.

JOHN HENRY CARDINAL NEWMAN

When we do the best that we can,
we never know what miracle is wrought
in our life, or in the life of another.

HELEN KELLER

*Nothing great was ever
achieved without enthusiasm.*

RALPH WALDO EMERSON

When love and skill work together,
expect a masterpiece.

JOHN RUSKIN

You are sowing the flowers of tomorrow
in the seeds of today.

UNKNOWN

Incline thine ear unto wisdom,
and apply thine heart to understanding.

PROVERBS 2:2

Your attitude about who you are and what you have is a very little thing that makes a very big difference.

THEODORE ROOSEVELT

God's grace keeps pace with whatever we face.

UNKNOWN

Love is most divine
when it loves according to needs,
and not according to merit.

GEORGE MACDONALD

While we try to teach our children
all about life, our children teach us
what life is all about.

ANONYMOUS

Finish each day and be done with it.
You have done what you could. . . .
Tomorrow is a new day; begin it well
and serenely and with too high a spirit
to be cumbered with your old nonsense.
This day is all that is good and fair. It is
too dear, with its hopes and invitations,
to waste a moment on yesterdays.

Ralph Waldo Emerson

Nothing is so strong as gentleness,
and nothing so gentle as real strength.

FRANCIS DE SALES

Whatsoever ye do, do it heartily,
as to the Lord, and not unto men.

COLOSSIANS 3:23

The greatest use of life is to spend it for something that will outlast it.

WILLIAM JAMES

Be on the lookout for mercies.
The more we look for them,
the more of them we will see.
Blessings brighten when we count them.

Maltbie D. Babcock

When you get into a tight place and everything goes against you, till it seems as though you could not hang on a minute longer, never give up then, for that is just the place and time that the tide will turn.

HARRIET BEECHER STOWE

A kind heart is a fountain of gladness,
making everything in its vicinity
freshen into smiles.

WASHINGTON IRVING

Every heart that has beat strong
and cheerfully has left a hopeful impulse
behind it in the world and bettered
the tradition of mankind.

ROBERT LOUIS STEVENSON

The main hope of a nation lies in the proper education of its youth.

ERASMUS

Worlds can be found by a child and an adult bending down and looking together under the grass stems or at the skittering crabs in a tidal pool.

ANONYMOUS

What we see depends mainly on what we look for.

JOHN LUBBOCK

When I approach a child,
he inspires in me two sentiments:
tenderness for what he is,
and respect for what he may become.

LOUIS PASTEUR

No pessimist ever discovered the secret
of the stars, or sailed to an uncharted land,
or opened a new doorway for the human spirit.

HELEN KELLER

How far you go in life depends on your being tender with the young, compassionate with the aged, sympathetic with the striving, and tolerant of the weak and the strong. Because someday in life you will have been all of these.

GEORGE WASHINGTON CARVER

A wise man will hear, and will increase learning; and a man of understanding shall attain unto wise counsels.

PROVERBS 1:5

The secret of education is respecting the pupil.

RALPH WALDO EMERSON

Rest is not idleness, and to lie sometimes
on the grass on a summer day listening
to the murmur of water, or watching
the clouds float across the sky,
is hardly a waste of time.

JOHN LUBBOCK

Bear in mind that the wonderful things you learn in your schools are the work of many generations. All this is put in your hands as your inheritance in order that you may receive it, honor it, add to it, and one day faithfully hand it on to your children.

ALBERT EINSTEIN

No dreamer is ever too small;
no dream is ever too big.

ANONYMOUS

Wake each morning with a sense of hope.
God has amazing things in store for you.
And He does all things well.

ELLYN SANNA

Daily duties are daily joys,
because they are something which God
gives us to offer unto Him, to do our
very best, in acknowledgment of His love.

EDWARD BOUVERIE PUSEY

My voice shalt thou hear in the morning, O LORD; in the morning will I direct my prayer unto thee, and will look up.

PSALM 5:3

*Don't let today's disappointments
cast a shadow on tomorrow's dreams.*

UNKNOWN

If you can bring one moment of happiness into the life of a child, you are a coworker with God.

COLLEEN L. REECE AND ANITA CORRINE DONIHUE

Be patient with everyone,
but above all with thyself. I mean,
do not be disheartened by your imperfections,
but always rise up with fresh courage.

FRANCIS DE SALES

Every day you shall wonder at yourself,
at the richness of life which has come
to you by the grace of God.

PHILLIPS BROOKS

Here I am, Lord—body, heart, and soul.
Grant that with Your love,
I may be big enough to reach the world,
and small enough to be at one with You.

MOTHER TERESA

The great opportunity is where you are.

JOHN BURROUGHS

Conditions are never just right.
People who delay action until all factors
are favorable are the kind who do nothing.

WILLIAM FEATHER

Keep away from people who try to belittle your ambitions. Small people always do that, but the really great make you feel that you, too, can become great.

MARK TWAIN

And this I pray, that your love may
abound yet more and more in
knowledge and in all judgment.

Philippians 1:9

The point is to develop the childlike inclination for play and the childlike desire for recognition and to guide the child over to important fields for society. Such a school demands from the teacher that he be a kind of artist in his province.

ALBERT EINSTEIN

Use what talents you possess;
the woods would be very silent if no
birds sang except those that sang best.

HENRY VAN DYKE

Education is not the filling of a pail, but the lighting of a fire.

WILLIAM BUTLER YEATS

Let us believe that God is in all our simple deeds and learn to find Him there.

A. W. TOZER

Yesterday is gone.
Tomorrow has not yet come.
We have only today. Let us begin.

MOTHER TERESA

Do what you can,
with what you have, where you are.

THEODORE ROOSEVELT

Teachers who inspire know that teaching is like cultivating a garden, and those who would have nothing to do with thorns must never attempt to gather flowers.

Unknown

Wherever a man turns,
he can find someone who needs him.

ALBERT SCHWEITZER

Learning is a treasure that will follow its owner everywhere.

CHINESE PROVERB

The world of tomorrow belongs to
the person who has the vision today.

ROBERT SCHULLER

Learning is not attained by chance;
it must be sought for with
ardor and diligence.

ABIGAIL ADAMS

A successful person is a dreamer whom someone believed in.

UNKNOWN

Praise does wonders
for the sense of hearing.

ANONYMOUS

Pleasant words are as an honeycomb,
sweet to the soul, and health to the bones.

PROVERBS 16:24

What we are is God's gift to us.
What we become is our gift to God.

ELEANOR POWELL

The heart is happiest when it beats for others.

UNKNOWN

If a man does not keep pace
with his companions, perhaps it is
because he hears a different drummer.
Let him step to the music he hears,
however measured or far away.

HENRY DAVID THOREAU

Do not let trifles disturb your tranquility of mind. . . . Life is too precious to be sacrificed for the nonessential and transient.

GLENVILLE KLEISER

We find in life exactly what we put into it.

RALPH WALDO EMERSON

The Constitution only gives people
the right to pursue happiness.
You have to catch it yourself.

BENJAMIN FRANKLIN

Everything that is done in this world is done by hope.

MARTIN LUTHER

It is today that your best work
can be done and not some
future day or future year.

UNKNOWN

Your heart is beating with God's love; open it to others. He has entrusted you with gifts and talents; use them for His service. He goes before you each step of the way; walk in faith. Take courage. Step out into the unknown with the One who knows all.

ELLYN SANNA

*Lord, help me to remember
the importance of the little things.*

COLLEEN L. REECE AND ANITA CORRINE DONIHUE

The whole art of teaching is only the art of awakening the natural curiosity of young minds for the purpose of satisfying it afterwards.

ANATOLE FRANCE

Who stops being better
stops being good.

Oliver Cromwell

Joy is the holy fire that keeps our purpose warm and our intelligence aglow. Work without joy is nothing.

HELEN KELLER

Life is a place of service, where one sometimes has occasion to put up with a lot that is hard, but more often to experience many joys.

LEO TOLSTOY

Every person you meet knows
something you don't.
Learn from them.

H. Jackson Brown Jr.

It is not enough to have a good mind.
The main thing is to use it well.

RENÉ DESCARTES

With God all things are possible.

MATTHEW 19:26

You cannot discover new oceans
unless you have the courage
to lose sight of the shore.

UNKNOWN

If I ran a school. . .I'd give the top grades to those who made a lot of mistakes and told me about them, and then told me what they learned from them.

R. BUCKMINSTER FULLER

Two roads diverged in a wood, and I—
I took the one less traveled by,
and that has made all the difference.

ROBERT FROST

Genius is undiscovered gold.
Talented is the teacher who struggles,
finds, and helps students develop it.

COLLEEN L. REECE AND ANITA CORRINE DONIHUE

As a general rule, teachers teach more
by what they are than by what they say.

ANONYMOUS

The real voyage of discovery consists
not in seeking new landscapes
but in having new eyes.

MARCEL PROUST

The secret of genius is to carry the spirit of the child into old age, which means never losing your enthusiasm.

ALDOUS HUXLEY

If Columbus had turned back, no one would have blamed him. Of course, no one would have remembered him, either.

UNKNOWN

If we work upon marble, it will perish;
if we work upon brass, time will efface it;
if we rear temples, they will crumble into dust;
but if we work upon immortal minds and
instill into them just principles, we are
then engraving that upon tablets which
no time will efface, but will brighten
and brighten to all eternity.

DANIEL WEBSTER

Do what you love.

HENRY DAVID THOREAU

Awaken people's curiosity.
It is enough to open minds;
do not overload them.
Put there just a spark.

ANATOLE FRANCE

Excellence can be attained if you care more than others think is wise, risk more than others think is safe, dream more than others think is practical, and expect more than others think is possible.

UNKNOWN

I consider a human soul without education like marble in the quarry, which shows none of its inherent beauties till the skill of the polisher fetches out the colors, makes the surface shine, and discovers every ornamental cloud, spot, and vein that runs through the body of it.

JOSEPH ADDISON

Father, help me never forget
the trust of a child is to be cherished.

PAMELA KAYE TRACY

The best teachers teach
from the heart, not from the book.

UNKNOWN

I am not a teacher, but an awakener.

Robert Frost

I will instruct thee and teach thee
in the way which thou shalt go.

PSALM 32:8

When you have exhausted all possibilities, remember this—you haven't.

THOMAS EDISON

The teacher is one who makes two ideas grow where only one grew before.

Elbert Hubbard

Do not train children to learning by force and harshness, but direct them to it by what amuses their minds, so that you may be better able to discover with accuracy the peculiar bent of the genius of each.

PLATO

*We all need someone who inspires us
to do better than we know how.*

ANONYMOUS

A word of encouragement during a failure is worth more than an hour of praise after success.

UNKNOWN

The door to success is labeled Push.

Oscar Wilde

A child's life is like a piece of paper
on which every passerby leaves a mark.

Chinese Proverb

*Life's aspirations come in
the guise of children.*

RABINDRANATH TAGORE

We cannot always build the future
for our youth, but we can build
our youth for the future.

FRANKLIN D. ROOSEVELT

My heart is singing for joy this morning.
A miracle has happened!
The light of understanding has shone
upon my little pupil's mind, and behold,
all things are changed.

ANNE SULLIVAN

We ourselves feel that what we are doing is just a drop in the ocean. But the ocean would be less because of that missing drop.

MOTHER TERESA

A professor can never better distinguish himself in his work than by encouraging a clever pupil, for the true discoverers are among them, as comets amongst the stars.

Carolus Linnaeus

Teaching is not a profession;
it's a passion.

UNKNOWN

There are three important qualities
of a good family. These are love,
cooperation, and positive expectations.
So it should be in a good school.

WILLIAM COOPER SMITH

Excellence is to do a common thing
in an uncommon way.

BOOKER T. WASHINGTON

He who has imagination without learning has wings and no feet.

JOSEPH JOUBERT

Any human anywhere will blossom
in a hundred unexpected talents and
capacities simply by being given
the opportunity to do so.

DORIS LESSING

*One's work may be finished someday,
but one's education never.*

ALEXANDER DUMAS

Every artist was at first an amateur.

RALPH WALDO EMERSON

Constant effort and frequent mistakes
are the stepping-stones of genius.

ELBERT HUBBÁRD

The beginning is the most important part of the work.

PLATO

Inspiration comes of working every day.

CHARLES BAUDELAIRE

Teaching is the highest form of understanding.

ARISTOTLE

Call unto me, and I will answer thee,
and shew thee great and mighty things,
which thou knowest not.

JEREMIAH 33:3

Fire starts with sparks.

UKRAINIAN PROVERB

Three grand essentials to happiness in this life are something to do, something to love, and something to hope for.

JOSEPH ADDISON

Wondrous is the strength of cheerfulness, and its power of endurance—the cheerful man will do more in the same time, will do it better, will preserve it longer, than the sad or sullen.

Thomas Carlyle

Education, in the broadest and truest sense, will make an individual seek to help all people, regardless of race, regardless of color, regardless of condition.

GEORGE WASHINGTON CARVER

Enthusiasm is contagious.
You can start an epidemic.

UNKNOWN

Flatter me, and I may not believe you.
Criticize me, and I may not like you.
Ignore me, and I may not forgive you.
Encourage me, and I may not forget you.

WILLIAM ARTHUR

It is the nature of man to rise to greatness
if greatness is expected of him.

JOHN STEINBECK

Blessed is the influence of one true,
loving human soul on another.

GEORGE ELIOT

He who influences the thought of his times influences the times that follow.

ELBERT HUBBARD

Hear instruction,
and be wise,
and refuse it not.

PROVERBS 8:33

He that planteth a tree...
provideth a kindness for many generations.

HENRY VAN DYKE

Three things in human life are important.
The first is to be kind.
The second is to be kind.
And the third is to be kind.

HENRY JAMES

Be the living expression of God's kindness: kindness in your face, kindness in your eyes, kindness in your smile.

MOTHER TERESA

Carve your names on hearts
and not on marble.

CHARLES H. SPURGEON

The spirited horse, which will try to
win the race of its own accord,
will run even faster if encouraged.

Ovid

Teaching should be such that what
is offered is perceived as a valuable gift
and not as a hard duty.

ALBERT EINSTEIN

Every thought which genius and piety throw into the world alters the world.

RALPH WALDO EMERSON

The best portion of a good man's life
is in his little nameless,
unremembered acts of kindness and of love.

WILLIAM WORDSWORTH

Without faith, nothing is possible.
With it, nothing is impossible.

MARY MCLEOD BETHUNE

Joy is prayer. Joy is strength. Joy is love. Joy is a net of love by which you can catch souls. She gives most who gives with joy.

MOTHER TERESA

As fast as each opportunity presents itself, use it! No matter how tiny an opportunity it may be, use it!

Robert Collier

Not knowing when the dawn will come, I open every door.

EMILY DICKINSON

A clever person turns great troubles
into little ones, and little ones
into none at all.

CHINESE PROVERB

Thy word is a lamp unto my feet,
and a light unto my path.

PSALM 119:105

I find my greatest pleasure, and so my reward, in the work that precedes what the world calls success.

THOMAS EDISON

To know how to suggest is the great art of teaching. To attain it we must be able to guess what will interest; we must learn to read the childish soul as we might a piece of music. Then, by simply changing the key, we keep up the attraction and vary the song.

HENRI-FRÉDÉRIC AMIEL

The greatest force in the world
is a positive idea.

ANONYMOUS

If we had no winter, the spring
would not be so pleasant; if we did not
sometimes taste adversity, prosperity
would not be so welcome.

ANNE BRADSTREET

I studied the lives of great men and famous women, and I found that the men and women who got to the top were those who did the jobs they had in hand, with everything they had of energy and enthusiasm.

HENRY TRUMAN

Act as if what you do makes a difference.
It does.

WILLIAM JAMES

Between tomorrow's dream and yesterday's regret is today's opportunity.

Unknown

Who questions much shall learn much, and retain much.

FRANCIS BACON

A loving heart is the truest wisdom.

CHARLES DICKENS

No one can look back on his schooldays
and say with truth that they were
altogether unhappy.

GEORGE ORWELL

A kind heart is a fountain of gladness, making everything in its vicinity freshen into smiles.

WASHINGTON IRVING

Godliness with contentment is great gain.

1 TIMOTHY 6:6

Seek joy in what you give.

UNKNOWN

How lovely to think that no one
need wait a moment, we can start now,
start slowly changing the world!

ANNE FRANK

I make the most of all that comes
and the least of all that goes.

SARA TEASDALE

Be an opener of doors.

RALPH WALDO EMERSON

Lives of great men all remind us
We can make our lives sublime,
And departing, leave behind us
Footprints on the sands of time.

HENRY WADSWORTH LONGFELLOW

If you have built castles in the air,
your work need not be lost;
that is where they should be.
Now put the foundations under them.

HENRY DAVID THOREAU

Nothing is worth more than this day.

JOHANN WOLFGANG VON GOETHE

Kind words are the music of the world.
They have a power which seems to
be beyond natural causes, as if they
were some angel's song which had lost
its way and come on earth.

FREDERICK WILLIAM FABER

Hope is like the sun, which,
as we journey toward it, casts the
shadow of our burden behind us.

SAMUEL SMILES

Ye shall know the truth,
and the truth shall make you free.

JOHN 8:32

Our work is meant to be a grace. It is a blessing and a gift, even a surprise and an act of unconditional love toward the community—and not just the present community that may or may not compensate us for our work, but the community to come, the generations that follow our work.

MATTHEW FOX

The marvelous richness of human experience would lose something of rewarding joy if there were no limitations to overcome. The hilltop hour would not be half so wonderful if there were no dark valleys to traverse.

HELEN KELLER

The young do not know enough to
be prudent, and therefore they attempt
the impossible—and achieve it.

PEARL S. BUCK

To find the universal elements enough;
to find the air and the water exhilarating;
to be refreshed by a morning walk or an
evening saunter. . .to be thrilled by the
stars at night; to be elated over a bird's nest
or a wildflower in spring—these are
some of the rewards of the simple life.

JOHN BURROUGHS

Always dream and shoot
higher than you know how to.
Don't bother just to be better than
your contemporaries or predecessors.
Try to be better than yourself.

WILLIAM FAULKNER

The purpose of life is a life of purpose.

ROBERT BYRNE

When we long for life without difficulties,
remind us that oaks grow strong in
contrary winds and diamonds
are made under pressure.

PETER MARSHALL

Commit thy works unto the Lord,
and thy thoughts shall be established.

PROVERBS 16:3

An optimist is a person who sees only
the lights in the picture, whereas a pessimist
sees only the shadows. An idealist, however,
is one who sees the light and the shadows,
but in addition sees something else: the
possibility of changing the picture, of making
the lights prevail over the shadows.

FELIX ADLER

Life is no brief candle to me.
It is a sort of splendid torch which I have
got a hold of for the moment, and I want
to make it burn as brightly as possible
before handing it on to future generations.

George Bernard Shaw